The Ballet Book

The Ballet Book

THE YOUNG PERFORMER'S GUIDE TO CLASSICAL DANCE

THE NATIONAL BALLET SCHOOL

WRITTEN AND ARRANGED BY DEBORAH BOWES

PRINCIPAL PHOTOGRAPHY BY LYDIA PAWELAK

FIREFLY BOOKS

A FIREFLY BOOK

Published by Firefly Books Ltd. 1999

First Printing

LIBRARY OF CONGRESS CATALOGUING IN PUBLICATION DATA

The ballet book / National Ballet School (Canada).
1st ed.
[144] p. : col. ill. ; cm.
Simultaneously published : Toronto : Key Porter Books, 1999.
Includes index and glossary.
Summary: How to begin in ballet and grow to be a happy dancer.
ISBN 1-55209-352-2
ISBN 1-55209-353-0 (pbk)
1. Ballet. 2. Ballet dancing. I. National Ballet School (Canada). II. Title.
798.8 / 071/ 09713 –dc21   1999   CIP

Published in the United States in 1999 by
Firefly Books (U.S.) Inc.
P.O. Box 1338, Ellicott Station
Buffalo, New York, USA
14205

Published in Canada in 1999 by Key Porter Books Limited.

Electronic formatting: Kathryn Moore
Design: Kathryn Moore

Printed and bound in Canada

Contents

Foreword

To celebrate my eighth birthday, my parents took me to see the National Ballet of Canada perform *Giselle*. Celia Franca, the company's founder, was a superb, dramatic dancer, and I was captivated by her performance in the leading role. This story of innocent first love, betrayal and forgiveness stole my heart. I knew then that I wanted to become a dancer. As I entered the National Ballet School, co-founded by Miss Franca and Betty Oliphant, my training began in earnest.

My dream did come true, and although not everyone will become a professional, all young dancers will develop many important skills. Whether they are dancing professionally, or just for fun, ballet training will enable them to explore their natural love of movement. The patience, discipline and determination learned in the studio can be applied to all future endeavours.

Ballet skills are passed on from one generation to the next by teachers who take great pleasure in sharing their knowledge and experience. This book can be used to complement a student's training, as it is an excellent resource for all young dancers, whether ballet is their sole passion or one of many interests. I know that I would have enjoyed this book as I was growing up. The pictures provide beautiful, clear examples of traditional ballet exercises, while always putting the joy of movement foremost.

My life in dance has been filled with exciting challenges and unimagined joys. I hope that all children who study ballet will find that, wherever their dance training leads, it always encourages their best efforts, brings them much happiness and gives them a lifelong appreciation of this wonderful art form.

Karen Kain
Artist in Residence,
The National Ballet of Canada

Preface

As Artistic Director of the National Ballet School, I was delighted to accept an invitation from Key Porter to produce a picture book for young dancers. As a member of the greater dance community, I realize that each of us plays an essential part in nurturing and celebrating this art form. While visiting schools across Canada and around the world, I am consistently inspired to see how ballet training strengthens bodies, improves coordination and sharpens minds: all skills that make us more fully aware of what the world has to offer.

As a teacher within a professional ballet school, where students aspire to careers in dance, I know that their dreams interconnect with the arts community as a whole. Our young dancers rely first and foremost on their parents' and teachers' support, and eventually on an enthusiastic and educated public.

Since you have opened the covers of this book, I anticipate that you, too, are drawn to dance. So whether you are just beginning your ballet training or are well into your journey, I assure you that this association will most definitely enliven and enrich your life.

Mavis Staines
Artistic Director,
Canada's National Ballet School

With many thanks to the exceptionally hard-working and enthusiastic young dancers who made this project possible.

Left to right: Phillip Blondon, Stefan Stewart, Elena Lobsanova, Jennifer Hynes, Tara Bhavnani, Guillaume Côté, Jillian Vanstone and Kiran West.

CHAPTER ONE

To Begin

Choosing to Dance

Many reasons draw students to ballet. Joy in movement, delight in make-believe, a desire to perform, or simply a love of music can make you wish for dance lessons. Attending an exciting ballet performance may inspire you to explore the world of dance. As ballet builds self-confidence, good posture and strong, limber muscles, your parents may suggest it. Health-care professionals realize that ballet may be beneficial to young persons with conditions such as scoliosis, or with a tendency to toe in, as it encourages them to work their bodies symmetrically, and with their legs rotated outwardly. Until the age of eight, children would benefit most from pre-ballet classes, emphasizing creative movement and eurythmics. At eight years or older, you are ready to adapt your body to the demands of classical dance.

Finding a Teacher

Once you have decided to take lessons, it is important to choose a teacher with care. Many teachers are members of the Imperial Society of Teachers of Dancing, which means that they have passed at least one teaching exam set by this international organization. Membership does not, however, guarantee good teaching, and you and your parent(s) should observe several classes before committing to lessons.

A strong dance background is essential for teaching. You need a teacher whose elegant use of upper body, arms and head will inspire you to develop your own sense of presentation. Although many excellent teachers have not danced professionally, a high degree of technical skill and artistry should be evident in their work. The teacher's students should be well focussed and hard-working, but free from undue tension or mannerisms. A good

teacher will be comfortable with the French terminology that is used to name all ballet steps. Be certain, also, that the teacher has a clear understanding of basic anatomy, to direct your training safely and effectively. Most of all, you need a teacher you feel comfortable with, one who creates a positive yet challenging atmosphere that allows you to work hard and enjoy expressing yourself through movement.

Musical Accompaniment

Music and dance have been entwined since the dawn of time, creating a form of self-expression fundamental to humankind. In the ballet class, a respectful, inspiring rapport between musician and teacher affirms the importance of musicality in movement. Choose a teacher who has studied music, can give rhythms clearly, tempi consistently, and whose voice expressively communicates musical qualities. The teacher's combinations of dance steps should be well phrased, and use a broad range of time signatures and musical forms.

An experienced musician (usually a pianist in today's ballet class) will play a wide variety of age-appropriate music, and be sensitive to the students' abilities, as well as to the dynamics and highlights of each exercise.

If the studio does not employ a musician, a large selection of recordings should be in use. Many excellent arrangements have been designed especially for the ballet class. A good musician is always preferable, however, as the interaction between pianist and dancer is fresh, adaptive and mutually supportive.

The Studio

The ideal studio would be large, airy and uniform in shape, although many teachers do outstanding work in less than ideal conditions. As ballet class begins at the *barre*, the studio should have *barres*, which are simply rounded lengths of wood, mounted roughly 30 centimetres from the wall, and 100 centimetres from the floor. Portable *barres* are also fine, especially in a space that is used for other activities, provided they are sufficiently weighted

and stable. You should be able to stand sideways to the *barre*, and easily kick your legs forward and backward without disturbing other students.

To ensure your safety when jumping, the floor should be sprung and finished in wood, vinyl or linoleum. A sprung floor has some give to it, which allows you to land from jumps without jarring yourself. Dancing on concrete is never a good idea.

Mirrors can be helpful, as they allow students to check their work, but young dancers should not focus on their mirror images throughout class, as this restricts the use of the head, and the development of line through the upper body. High ceilings are also a plus, both practically and psychologically.

Finally, it is important that the temperature in the studio be well regulated, in order to allow the dancers' muscles to warm up easily and then stay pliable throughout class.

What to Wear

Dancers may perform in elegant, often elaborate costumes; however, for class you need simple, close-fitting clothing that has been especially designed for ease of movement. Girls wear a snug leotard—a bodysuit designed by

Monsieur Léotard more than a century ago—so that the teacher can check posture at a glance. A sleeveless leotard is a good idea, as it will keep you and your teacher mindful of the line of your shoulders.

Bare legs, with short socks, will allow you to first recognize, and then use, your leg muscles correctly. When tights are worn, they must also be carefully fitted to hug the legs, and not restrict movement. Pink tights are the best choice for girls, as the light colour allows muscle actions and lines to remain clearly visible. Boys usually wear shorts or tights over a leotard, or with a T-shirt, when they are starting out. A unitard, with its uncluttered lines, is another option. Boys also need an athletic support (called a dance belt), and an elasticized belt to hold up their tights.

Boys and girls both need special ballet slippers, which are generally made from canvas or soft leather. They should fit the feet exactly, supporting their shape without allowing any extra "room to grow." You will then be able to see and feel your feet develop strength and flexibility. Elastic, or ribbons sewn securely to the sides of the slipper, will keep it molded to your foot. Sew them where the back of the shoe touches the side when it is

folded forward from the sole. Avoid catching the outside of the slipper, or the drawstring, in your stitches. To keep your ballet slippers clean and to prevent the soles from becoming slippery, wear them only when you are inside the studio.

Most girls look forward to going on pointe; however, this does not happen until, after several years of study, your teacher feels you are strong enough. Under their beautiful satin exteriors, pointe shoes have a hard shell made from layers of burlap and glue. You will need guidance from an experienced pointe shoe fitter to find the shoes that best suit your feet, as there are many options available.

Your teacher may also suggest some warm-up clothing to wear while waiting for class, or on chilly days. Close-fitting woolen leg warmers or a cotton sweatsuit are probably best, as they absorb perspiration, rather than trapping it close to the skin. Be certain to discuss all clothing purchases in advance with your teacher, as many schools ask their students to wear specific styles and colours. Remember that snug, simple clothing is best, as it allows you to check your positions and become comfortable with your physique.

Grooming

Good grooming contributes to the development of self-discipline and attention to detail, attributes that are essential in the making of an artist. In classical ballet, the line of the neck and the carriage of the head are very important. Boys' hair should be kept short, or tied back, while girls with short hair need a hairband or clips to keep their hair back. Girls with long hair should wear it up in a bun. Begin your bun with a high ponytail, so that it will follow the line of your cheekbones. Twist your ponytail, and then coil it tightly around the elastic. Use a hairnet and hairpins to secure your bun. Jewelry and watches should not be worn in the studio, as they could come loose during vigorous movements, and become a hazard to you or your classmates.

CHAPTER TWO

Ballet Class

The pictures in this book are identified by the terminology presently in use at the National Ballet School. At your studio you may use some different terms, perhaps from the Cecchetti or Royal Academy of Dancing syllabi. These terms are equally legitimate, and although the names may differ, what they seek to achieve is the same the world over. Your arms, for example, should frame your body with elegance, whether the position is called *fifth en bas* (Cecchetti), *bras bas* (RAD), or *preparatory* (Vaganova). As you study these pictures you may find that you have been instructed to position yourself somewhat differently. In good training, however, the similarities are always profound, while the differences ensure a rich variety of style and expression.

Positions of the Arms

Pictured here are four basic
positions. In your ballet class you will
learn many more, and will come to
see how a subtle change in the use of
your head, or the angle of your arm,
can completely alter the spirit of the
position.

Preparatory Position

Frame your well-centred body with
a softly curved oval. Let the tops of
your arms snuggle back in the
shoulder sockets and bring your
elbows slightly forward, in front of
the side seams of your leotard. Feel
the energy that reaches across the
gap between your fingers and
connects each finger with its twin on
the other hand.

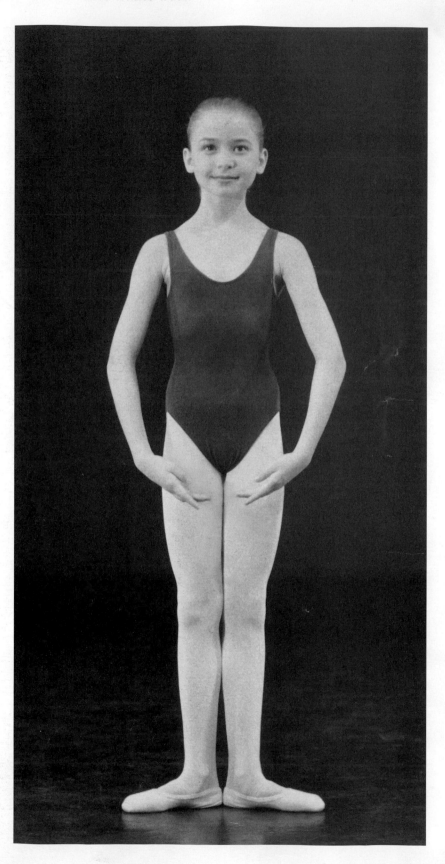

First Position

Lift your preparatory oval in line with your centre, while keeping the tops of your arms and your shoulders calm and relaxed. This pivotal position can be used as a gateway to other arm positions or maintained for a variety of reasons, such as to stabilize turning movements.

Second Position

Reach your arms out into a generous, open line that slopes slightly down from your shoulders. Keep your elbows buoyant and your arms gently curved, as if to include the entire audience in a welcoming embrace.

Third Position

Lift your preparatory oval to frame your face. Once again, relax your shoulders as you lift from under your arms. Check that your third fingers softly follow the line of the oval, while your thumbs relax toward them to complement this line.

Positions of the Feet

The position of the foot is determined by the rotation of the top of the thigh bone in the hip socket. Always turn out to your maximum, but never clench your feet or roll them forward. Keep an equal amount of weight on your little and big toe metatarsals (the balls of the feet). Remember that the rotation of your feet will increase as your turnout muscles strengthen.

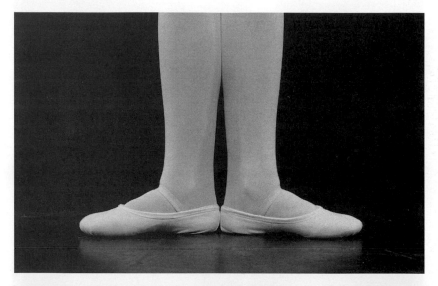

First Position

With your heels touching, stand in your best turnout. Let your feet melt into the floor to give your dancing secure roots.

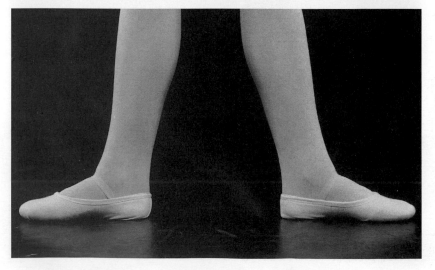

Second Position

Keep the turnout you established in first position, and stand with your heels aligned under your shoulders. Your teacher will help you determine the exact width that best suits your physique.

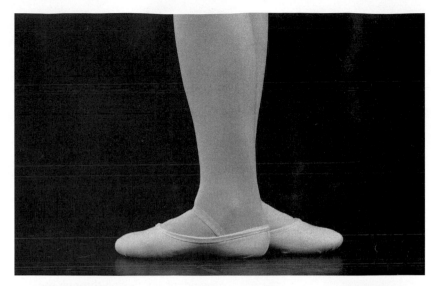

Third Position

Cross one foot to the middle of the other. Check that your hips are centred equally over your feet, and not allowed to twist forward or back in sympathy with them.

Fourth Position

Here your feet are crossed, as in fifth position, but they are separated by approximately one foot length. In this advanced position, you must work hard to centre your hips between your feet, and equalize your turnout and weight placement.

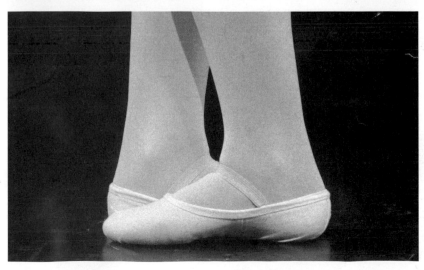

Fifth Position

When you can stand correctly and work well from first position, your teacher will probably move your home base to third, and finally to fifth position. You may begin fifth with your front heel crossing to the big toe joint of your back foot, and then gradually increase this crossing action as your technique strengthens.

Cou-de-Pied Positions

In these positions, your gesture foot is placed elegantly at the ankle of your standing leg. It can be relaxed or fully stretched. It can be fixed at the front or back of the supporting ankle, or wrapped around it. When stretched, your foot should be sickled out. This means that the heel is presented well forward, while avoiding any flexion through the ankle.

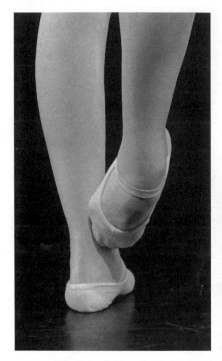

Conditional Cou-de-Pied

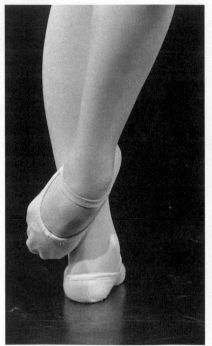

Cou-de-Pied Devant

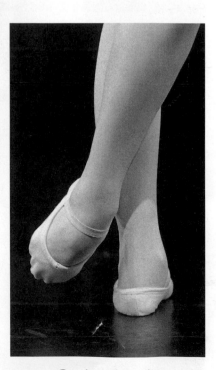

Cou-de-Pied Derrière

Positions of the Body

To develop your own sense of spacing, and to create harmony of line in group work, imagine that you are at the centre of a small square as you dance. You can then visualize your positions correctly, regardless of where you are on stage. Always relate your studio to the stage.

En Face

This alignment, where you face directly out to the audience, is simple yet engaging. If you were now to move forward, toward your teacher or audience, you would be travelling downstage. Stages used to be raked (sloped) in order to afford the audience, which was seated on one level, a better view of the performers. Even today, we refer to the back and front of the stage as upstage and downstage.

Croisé

By facing a downstage corner of
your imaginary square, you present
yourself in a sophisticated and
flattering alignment. This is
sometimes referred to as using
épaulement. When, from the point of
view of the audience, your
downstage leg crosses your upstage
leg, you are standing *en croisé*.

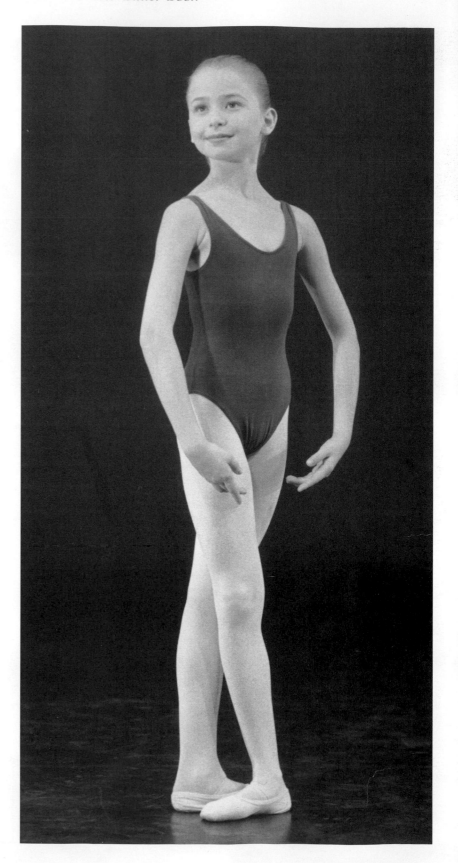

Effacé

This *ouvert* or uncrossed alignment
has an ethereal, weightless quality.
Imagine that a light illuminates you
in part, and casts a soft shadow over
the rest of your body. Lift your
upstage cheek to the light, as if to
bask in its glow.

At the Barre

Your class will probably last for one or one-and-a-half hours. It should be divided into three fairly equal parts, with the *barrework* taking up the first third of the class. In these exercises, one or both hands rest lightly on the *barre* as you warm up, and work at developing your basic technique.

Standing Ready in First and Fifth Positions

Clear your mind of other thoughts, and focus on the task ahead. Centre and lengthen your spine; place your weight equally over both feet, and engage your abdominal and turnout muscles. You are now well on the way to developing the *aplomb* (stable vertical alignment) that is essential in dance.

Demi-Plié in First Position

Sustain your turnout, but relax through your ankle, knee and hip joints as you direct your knees over your second toes. Bend as much as you can without losing the downward pressure through your heels, or distorting your spinal alignment. Do not stop at the depth of your *plié*, as a round *demi-plié* is the key to good *allegro* work.

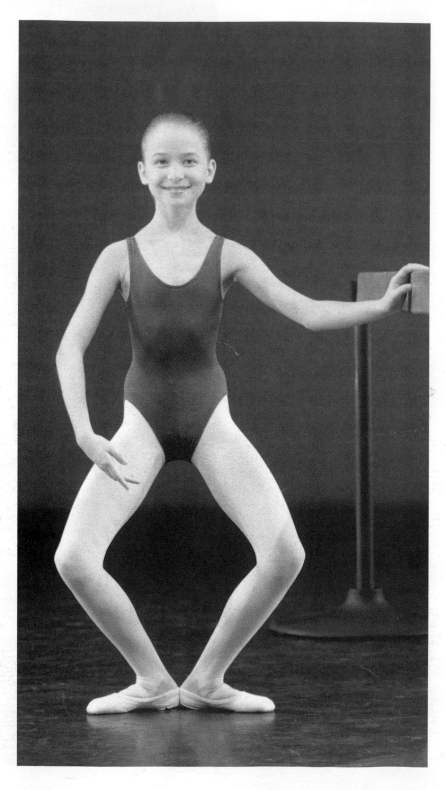

Grand Plié in Fifth Position

As your knees continue to bend, your heels will be forced to peel away from the floor. Keep your hips on top of your thighs and directly over your feet, even at the depth of your *plié*. Then let the smooth, downward thrust of your heels bring you up again. When done correctly, *grand pliés* will warm up and strengthen your legs.

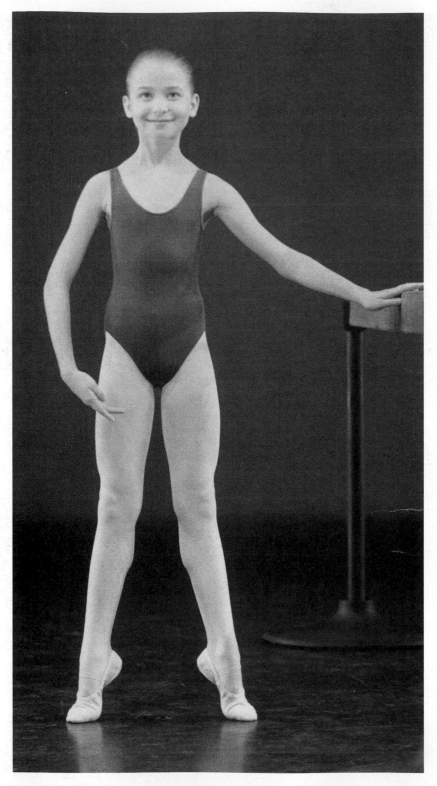

Relevé in First Position

Keep your toes relaxed, and press up onto the balls of your feet. Work through the centre of your feet and ankles, and maintain your turnout. *Relevés* will strengthen your legs, ankles and feet, and along with *pliés*, they form the building blocks of dance.

Battement Tendu à la Seconde

Begin by sliding your heel along the floor, and then work smoothly through your foot until it is fully stretched. Keep your hips lifted and level, while turning out your standing and gesture legs equally.

Battements tendus develop strength and flexibility in your feet and ankle joints. They also teach you to pinpoint the three basic positions: *à la seconde*, *devant*, and *derrière*.

Battement Tendu Devant

Lead forward with your heel and keep it well-presented as you stretch your foot. To close, lead back with your toes. Remember that the instant your gesture leg moves from fifth position, your body weight is sustained solely by your standing leg. Lift well through your supporting hip and thigh, in order to maintain the vertical alignment of your weight-bearing leg, so that this adjustment is discreet.

Battement Tendu Derrière

Turn out both legs vigorously, stretch
the back of your gesture knee, and
do not disturb the placement of your
tailbone as you begin the *tendu
derrière*. While keeping the lift in your
spine, right through to the top of
your head, glance into the palm of
your hand. Always use your eyeline
to extend your line of dance. Here,
you are drawing the audience into
your movement. More usually,
however, your eye focus reaches out
to engage the audience.

Battement Tendu Jeté à la Seconde

With a quick, energetic action, brush through the *battement tendu* movement to a point just off the floor. This brisk, light movement allows your feet to develop a rapid response to the floor: just what is needed in *petit allegro* work.

Rond de Jambe par Terre

Use this exercise to maximize your turnout and develop your understanding of *en dehors* (outward) and *en dedans* (inward) movements. As your gesture leg inscribes a semi-circle, work to increase its rotation in the hip socket.

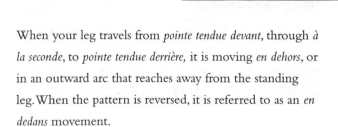

When your leg travels from *pointe tendue devant*, through *à la seconde*, to *pointe tendue derrière,* it is moving *en dehors*, or in an outward arc that reaches away from the standing leg. When the pattern is reversed, it is referred to as an *en dedans* movement.

To benefit most from this exercise, keep your standing leg active and your hand on the *barre* relaxed. Throughout class, even when concentrating on a specific task, stay alert to the alignment of your body as a whole.

Battement Fondu à la Seconde

This smooth, sustained step emphasizes coordination and phrasing. As you simultaneously bend and then stretch both knees, you are laying the foundation for powerful *allegro* work. To begin, extend your gesture leg at a 45-degree angle from the floor.

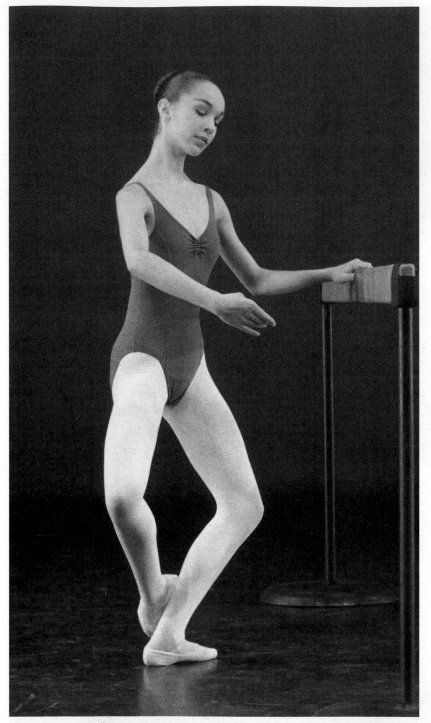

Battement Fondu Derrière

In this more advanced version, you travel through a broader range of movement to finish on a *relevé*, in a 90-degree extension. To further advance your coordination, phrase your *port de bras* exactly with your legwork.

Battement Frappé

In this quick, staccato action of the lower leg, your toes and the ball of your foot skip along the floor, launching your foot and ankle into a strongly pointed position. This movement activates the intrinsic muscles of your foot and teaches it how to respond to the floor for quick jumps and pointe work.

Be careful not to jar your knee joint as you stretch your leg and foot as quickly as possible. Point your toes forcefully, and hold each extension as long as the music will allow. Keep a light touch on the *barre* to ensure that you are gaining the strength to transfer these exercises into the centre.

Petit Battement

Here an easy, relaxed knee joint lets your thigh and lower leg act independently. Keep your thigh well turned out as your foot moves slightly sideways and then back into alternating *cou-de-pied* positions.

Present your lower leg and foot with
finesse. Your teacher will increase the
repetitions, and the speed at which
you perform your *petits battements*, as
you master this movement and are
able to keep your knee free of tension.

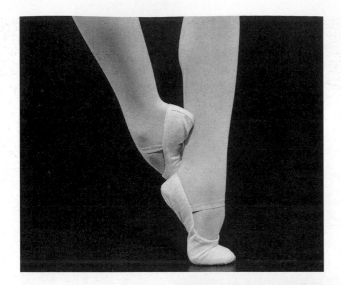

Your footwork in *petits battements* should be crisp, vivid and exact. Whether travelling from front to back, or in reverse, always pinpoint your sideways action to touch the same spot *en l'air*.

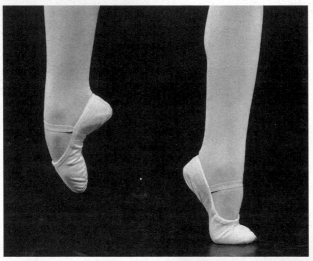

Passé Devant

When taken as an *adage* movement, the *passé* is gracefully balanced and finely controlled. Let the top of your thigh rotate and release to the bottom of the hip socket as you lift under the knee and elegantly draw your toes up your standing leg.

Développé Devant

From *passé devant*, lead forward with
your heel, maximizing your turnout
and stretching your gesture leg into
an extension *devant*. Ensure that you
maintain or increase the height of
your thigh as your leg unfolds into
this position. Let your eyeline
reinforce your legwork by reaching
from a soft, introspective feeling in
passé to a radiant, outgoing
extension.

Développé Ecarté Derrière

Turn slightly away from the barre, lift through *passé*, and extend into *à la seconde* in one smooth, continuous action. When you perform these movements on a *relevé*, they become even more challenging. Turn your head proudly and look diagonally down to colour this pose correctly.

Arabesque Penchée

Arabesque is often called the longest and most elegant line in dance. It can be dazzling whether your gesture leg is placed *à terre*, or taken to its full height *en l'air*. When performing an *arabesque penchée*, the lift under the thigh of your gesture leg tilts your body and arm forward into a complementary line. During this movement, your standing leg must remain taut, and function as a strong vertical axis.

Grand Battement

Brush your gesture foot along the floor, toss it freely and lightly in an upward arc, and lower it with control through *pointe tendue*. This action develops both flexibility and strength as you strive for ever higher extensions while maintaining a well-held centre and secure standing leg. The quick throwing action also contributes to powerful takeoffs in *grand allegro* work, and the controlled lowering promotes cushioned landings.

Bends

You need to be limber, yet securely centred, in order to master the many bends required in ballet. Bends can be taken sideways, forward, backward, or even in a circular motion. They may be subtle or expansive gestures, serene or dramatic in quality. They can be used to connect steps, or to punctuate the end of a phrase of movement. When bending, keep an image of the line of your entire body uppermost in your mind.

In the Centre

Coming into the centre, you will now repeat many of the movements first taken at the *barre*. This will further develop your sense of *aplomb* and secure your technique. You will also perform *port de bras, pirouettes, adage* and *allegro* work. The study of *port de bras* focusses on the positions of the arms, and on the flowing circles of movement that link these positions. Use your upper body, head and arms in harmony with each other, and in coordination with the rest of your body, to make your dancing cohesive. *Pirouettes* belong to a larger family of turns that are practised on their own and then incorporated throughout your classwork. In *adage*, you will concentrate on slow, graceful movements usually performed while balancing on one leg. Sense of line, movement quality, and use of dynamics are highlighted in this area of your training.

Your class will culminate in the study of *allegro*, where jumps and travelling steps will provide you with immensely satisfying challenges. Here everything you have learned is combined in what is considered by many to be the essence of classical dance.

Port de Bras

Translated literally, *port de bras* means carriage of the arms. Even at its most basic, however, *port de bras* integrates your upper body, head, and breath with your arm movements.

3

Let your fingertips draw broad,
flowing circles of movement in the
space around you as they reach into
and lift out of the positions found in
this *port de bras.*

4

Classical Ballet Poses

Croisé Devant

When you have mastered the basic arm and leg positions, and can stand confidently in both *croisé* and *effacé* alignments, you are ready to study the poses of classical ballet. These six poses are fundamental to the language of dance. To begin, your gesture foot is placed *à terre*, and then later, to fully develop the big poses, it is taken *en l'air*. When performing smaller steps, such as *petit allegro*, the small poses best balance your legwork. In these poses, a low first position of the arm is substituted for third.

Croisé Devant
&
Croisé Derrière

In these bright, vivacious poses, the lines of movement formed by your arms, legs and head reach energetically across each other. A clear sense of placement, from your torso to your extremities, allows these positions to sparkle.

Effacé Devant

A single sweeping curve arcs through these poses, giving them a gentle, uplifting quality. Although each pose affords many possibilities for self-expression, *effacé*, by design, is light and aerial.

Effacé Derrière

The breadth of line in *écarté* demands a proud and noble bearing. Imagine that your profile is to be engraved on a coin to symbolize honour and magnanimity.

Ecarté Derrière

Ecarté Devant

Arabesques

This long, flowing line, reaching from the fingertips of your front hand to the ends of your pointed toes, is enhanced by the line of your back arm, and extended by your eyeline. In first *arabesque*, turn your gesture leg *en dehors*, and spiral your ribcage in the opposite direction. Third *arabesque* offers an excellent starting point from which to explore the complexities of this position.

First Arabesque

Second Arabesque

As you gain strength, *arabesques* are taken *en l'air*. Lift strongly through your abdominal and lower back muscles to achieve the graceful upward curve that is distinctive to this position. Keep your shoulders relaxed and level, and your fingertips sensitive to the line you are sculpting through your arms and upper back.

Fourth Arabesque

Here, the legs are positioned exactly as in third *arabesque*; however, the opposite arm is brought forward, and the upstage spiral of the torso adds dynamic interest. Feel the upward momentum of the spiral, as your back is turned to the audience, and balance it with a vigorous, outward rotation of your standing leg. This is the most challenging of the four *arabesques*.

Attitudes

This pose appears to enclose space, as the gesture leg sweeps around the axis formed by your raised arm, torso and standing leg. The gesture knee should be well-crossed, fully rotated and lifted above the heel. Carlo Blasis originated this pose in the 1800s. A famous dancer and teacher in Milan, he was so inspired by Jean de Boulogne's statue of Mercury that he incorporated its form into a ballet. *Attitudes* may be performed both *devant* and *derrière*, and in a variety of alignments.

Attitude Croisé Derrière

Turning Steps

Turning is an exhilarating sensation which you have probably been exploring ever since you could walk. Do you remember spinning around in a playground, arms outstretched, until you collapsed, dizzy and happy? The enjoyment and challenge continue in ballet class, where many steps can be done *en tournant* and some, such as *pirouettes* and *tours en l'air*, are designed exclusively for turning.

To turn without becoming dizzy, keep your head still and your eyes focussed on something directly in front of you as you begin to turn your body. Then whip your head around, at a rate faster than your body, to focus again on exactly the same spot. Dancers call this whipping action of the head "spotting." Listen carefully to the music, as it will help you to spot rhythmically and turn with ease. To perform multiple turns, remain focussed on your spot, but only delay the whipping action of your head on the initial turn.

Pirouettes

Single Pirouette en Dehors

These are turns performed on one leg, with the gesture foot secured in a *passé* position. Later, in *grandes pirouettes*, you will turn in a wide variety of poses. To turn successfully, lift through your spine as you breathe out

into a well organized *demi-plié*. Then press strongly away from the floor, coordinating your arm and leg movements to arrive simultaneously in pirouette position. Lightly whip your head around to find your

spot and gauge your force, in order to control your turn. Always finish up, securely balanced on your vertical axis, and then lift into your final pose with finesse. *Pirouettes* start and finish in many positions, but always revolve either *en dehors* or *en dedans*. When turning *en dehors*, the turnout of your gesture leg initiates the turn, while in *en dedans* movements, this strategy is reversed.

Tours en l'air

Single Tour en l'Air

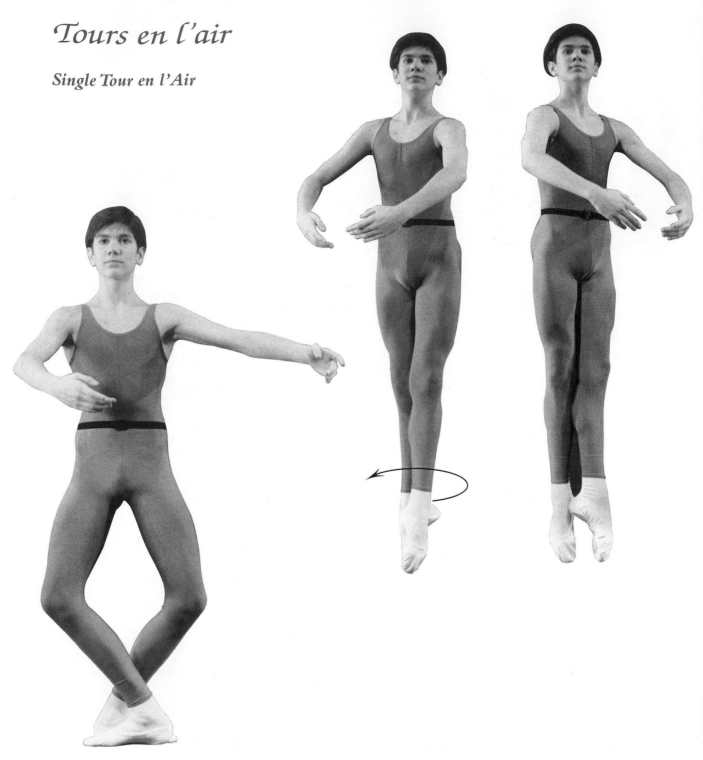

These turns are performed in the air. When you can take off and land from jumps in a well-aligned *plié*, and maintain your posture correctly in the air, your teacher will most likely introduce quarter and then half *tours* as a build-up to full *tours*. Basic *tours* start and finish on two feet, while more advanced variations include *tours* in *passé* position and in

the poses. Generally, both boys and girls learn single *tours*, while boys go on to study double and even triple *tours*. Use a quick spotting head movement, and keep your vertical axis intact, from the tips of your toes to the very top of your head, as you practise this step. Good postural alignment should allow you to finish with *aplomb*.

Petit Allegro

Jumps play a big part in our lives. From catching a ball to crossing a puddle, we depend on jumps to extend our range of motion. The classical ballet repertoire is full of exciting jumps, and you will meet them in the *allegro* (Italian for "brisk and lively") section of your class.

Petit allegro steps are practised first, then medium, and finally *grand allegro* movements are studied. Initially when jumping, you will push off from and land on both feet. As you develop a strong technical base, you will take on the challenge of more complex *allegro* steps. Your legwork and *port de bras* should always make a picture at the top of each jump, allowing you to appear suspended *en l'air* for a brief but glorious moment.

Temps Levé in First Position

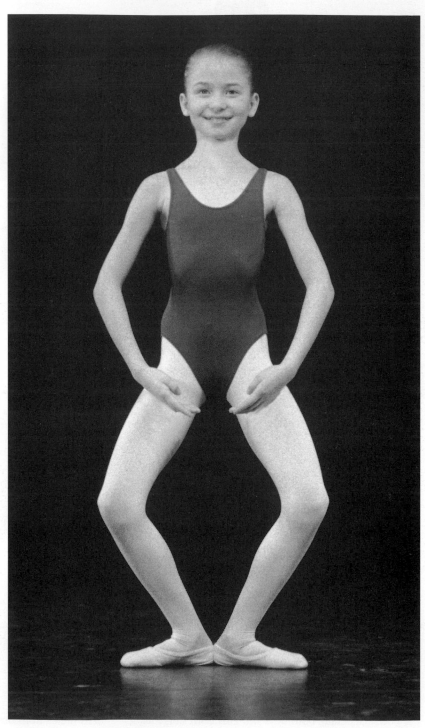

Release your feet, ankles, knees and hip joints into a spongy demi-plié.

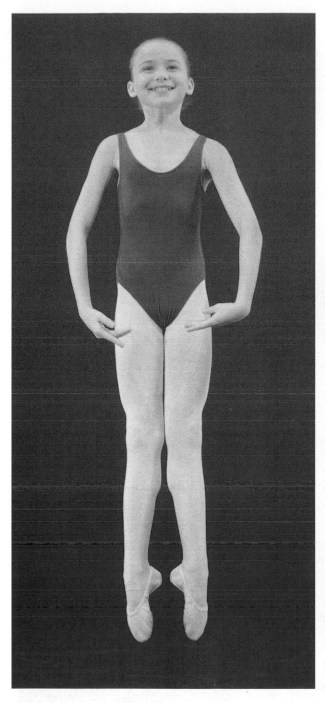

*Engage your foot and leg muscles
to push quickly and strongly away from the floor.*

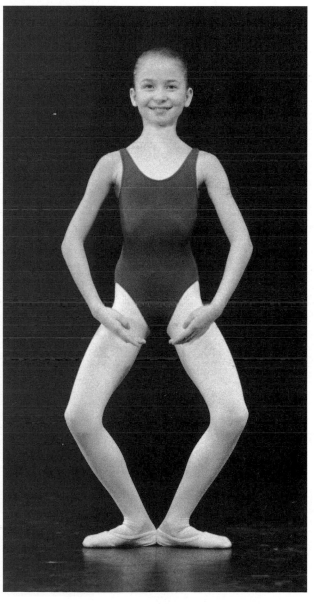

*Land lightly, toes first, on the same spot and in the same
cushiony plié.*

*Temps Levé in
Second Position*

Use the circular action of your plié *to rocket into the air.*

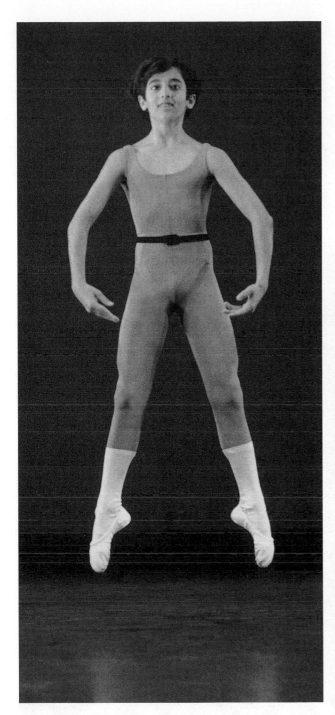

Point your feet as forcefully as possible, to help you pause at the top of the jump.

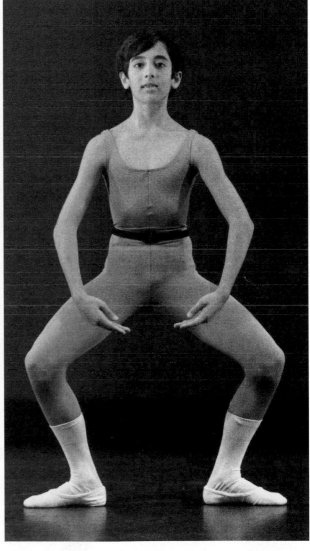

Lift through your centre so that you can control your plié.

Temps Levé in Fifth Position

In *petit allegro* steps, you can be
challenged to jump as high as possible,
or to make your movements *terre à
terre* (low and close to the floor). The
music may suggest that you balance
the time you spend *à terre* and *en l'air*,
or push you to rebound quickly from
your *pliés* and spend as much time as
possible in the air.

For fun and stamina, your teacher may challenge you to find new positions *en l'air*. For example, you may bend your knees under you or stretch them into the splits as you jump. These skills will be useful later on as you explore the more complex *allegro* steps. Right now, visualize the perfect position *en l'air* and aim for it in each takeoff.

Petit Echappé Sauté

In this step, connect your jumps with
a full, rebounding and musical use of
your *demi-plié*. Your toes should act
like fine-tipped markers, drawing
perfect arches in the air as you
"escape" from fifth to second or
fourth position and then return
home.

Melt through your feet into your
best *demi-plié* in *à la seconde* position.
Fly exactly to, and not past, this spot.

When you finish this movement,
with the opposite foot in front in
fifth position, you have performed a
petit échappé changé. *Echappés* may also
be taken *sans changé*. Later you will
learn *grand échappés*, as well as *échappés*
that finish on one leg in any number
of interesting poses.

Batterie

Entrechat Quatre

When, in *allegro* work, your turnout
is well maintained, both *à terre* and *en
l'air*, you may progress to *batterie* or
beaten steps. After preparatory drills
have trained your legs to beat across
each other and against the air, you
can focus on *échappé battu* and the
basic *entrechats*. In time you will
increase the tempo of your beats to
perform brilliant *terre à terre batterie*,
and decrease it to develop virtuoso
grand allegro batterie.

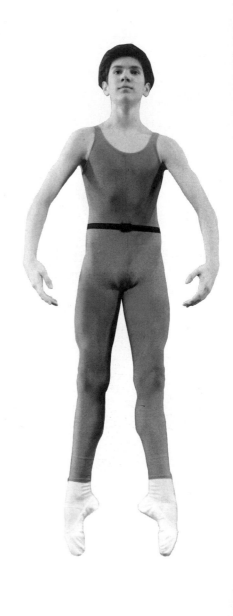

*Divide your weight exactly between both
feet, to ensure an equal action en l'air.*

*Push your insteps toward a very
small second position as you take off.*

Cross your fifth position as much as possible, while sustaining your turnout.

Rebound into the same, or a slightly wider position.

Avoid overcrossing in fifth as you land.

Medium Allegro

The numerous *allegro* steps that fall into this category are important both as repertoire in their own right, and as a bridge to *grand allegro*. The skills you have already established, such as a well-aligned and rhythmical use of *plié*, and an easy coordination of arm and leg movements, are essential to a healthy and artistic execution of these demanding jumps.

Passé Sauté

From an elastic *plié* in fifth, spring energetically into a clear and well-composed picture at the height of your jump. While one leg thrusts strongly downward, the other darts into *passé* position. Remember to coordinate these movements with your *port de bras*. To finish, land on two feet, simultaneously, in a resilient *demi-plié*.

Assemblé Porté

Assemblés are done *sur place*, and then travelled, as the technique of brushing one foot against the floor and then lifting both legs into fifth, at the top of the jump, is mastered.

Always incorporate your head and eyeline into your *port de bras* and extend this line as you land, to give the impression of staying longer *en l'air*.

Balancés

Balancés travel from side to side, forward and back, and *en tournant* in generous, elegant movements. In all instances, your centre should reach through space in a rainbow shaped arc while your *port de bras* ebbs and flows with the music.

The lyrical *balancé* is often found in *allegro enchaînements,* danced to grand and sweeping waltzes. *Balancés,* however, can take on a completely different character depending on the music—becoming, for example, bright and bouncy when done to a lively mazurka.

Grand Allegro

In *grand allegro* all your hard work comes together to let you soar *en l'air* in *enchaînements* that paint the entire stage with broad, electrifying strokes of movement. A fluid and classical use of *port de bras* must operate in harmony with powerful leg and footwork, to achieve the fusion of artistry and athleticism required by *grand allegro*, in particular. Work with the music, and it will lend you wings; work against it, and you will be weary and earthbound.

Learn to visualize each *enchaînement* as a whole before dancing it. Note its structure, use of dynamics and highlights. Make use of the images suggested by your teacher, or find your own, to lend intent and clarity to your movement.

To develop quality *allegro* work, it is also important to grasp the concept of landings as takeoffs. A well-aligned and resilient *plié* will keep the momentum of an exercise going, and allow you to build fluid movement phrases. This light, rebounding quality that is needed to link steps together is often referred to as *ballon*.

Grand Jeté en Avant

Linking steps—*glissades* or *pas couru* for example—can be used as a springboard to large jumps, such as *grand jetés*. Although there are many types of *jetés*, they all take off from one leg and land on the other. A *grand jeté en avant* may highlight elevation, horizontal leg action, or both. Regardless of the shape of the movement, keep your torso poised above your legs *en l'air*, and well lifted as you land. Keep in mind that panther-like landings appear easy, but in fact require strenuous muscle work. A practice tutu allows girls to experience the effect of a costume on their movements prior to performing.

On Pointe

Pointe shoes were a natural outcome of the romantic movement, as they enabled women to take on the weightless, ethereal quality desired by the choreographers of the day. In both *La Sylphide* (1832) and *Giselle* (1841), female dancers portrayed otherworldly creatures, unfettered by gravity and as elusive as the air around them. At first, dancers simply posed *sur les pointes* from time to time, but today's dancers perform an increasingly large and demanding repertoire on pointe.

Most girls are impatient to go on pointe. Principled teachers will not, however, suggest it until you are well prepared. You should have excellent control of your centre and spinal alignment, strong leg and footwork, and balance easily on *demi-pointe* before you begin pointe. In addition, a commitment to more than one ballet class a week is essential.

When the magic day does arrive, your pointe shoes will need expert fitting. In addition to being the right size, options such as the flexibility of the shank, cut of the vamp, and shape of the block must be considered. Rely on your teacher to show you how to break in your shoes, and keep your feet healthy. You may be asked to darn the blocks of your pointe shoes to make them less slippery or to shellac them so that they last longer. Dancers often wrap a bit of padding, such as lambswool or adhesive tape, around their toes for comfort. To toughen up skin prone to blisters, massage your feet regularly with a little rubbing alcohol or witch hazel. Open blisters must be kept clean, and covered with an antibiotic ointment and bandage or gel-like dressing. If you have any structural irregularities that could cause discomfort on pointe, such as a slanting big toe or a long second toe, your teacher will help you to align your toes with such tricks of the trade as foam spacers, or individual toe caps. Not every girl is physically suited to pointe work, but if your teacher thinks that you may be, it should not be a painful experience.

After learning how to prepare your feet and shoes, and secure your ribbons in an invisible knot behind your ankle bone, you are set for pointe class. The first lessons will probably occur during the final fifteen minutes of your ballet class, and include such basic movements as walks and *tendus*. This will encourage you to use your feet as sensitively and articulately as you do in soft slippers. When you finally step up onto pointe, in sixth position, stand squarely on the ends of your shoes and extend your postural plumb line into the centre of each block. Lift well through your hips, legs and feet to avoid sinking into your shoes and bruising your toes. After finding the correct position on pointe, your next challenge will be to move seamlessly on and off pointe in both pressed and sprung *relevés*.

Working on pointe lengthens the line of your leg, extends your range of movement and adds to the potential for virtuosity. Most of all, when well controlled and performed noiselessly, it imparts a graceful, aerial quality to your dancing.

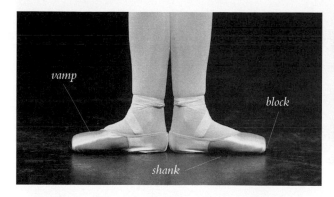

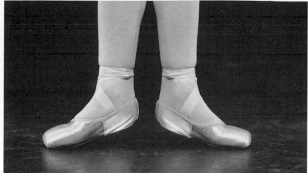

Quarter Pointe

Half Pointe

Three-Quarter Pointe

Full Pointe

Relevé in First Position

Peel your feet smoothly away from the floor as you roll up onto pointe. The three main positions you will pass through are quarter, half and three-quarter pointe. Quick *relevés* demand a more rapid response to the floor and when performing them, you should arrive on full pointe in the blink of an eye.

Relevé en Attitude Croisée Derrière

After securing your *relevés* on two feet, you may *relevé* onto one foot from two feet, and finally, from one foot onto the same foot. You can *relevé* from a *demi-plié* or straight legs, and stay *sur place* or travel as you press up onto pointe. In these *relevés*, ensure that your gesture foot reaches *passé* position, or arrives *en attitude,* at the same moment that you arrive on pointe.

Ballet demands strong, supple footwork. Your feet need to be wonderfully expressive, and yet they must support you without fail. Always pause for a moment on pointe, as if to float suspended above the floor, even during quick movements.

Relevé Devant

Relevé en Attitude Croisée Devant

Branching Out

Your training may include classes in such closely related and complementary subjects as historical or character dance, mime and partnering. Both historical dance and character are rooted in folk dance, which became stylized after passing through the hands of ballet masters and choreographers, and was incorporated into many classical ballets. You should know the language of mime, as ballet contains many formalized gestures that you need to recognize and become able to use fluently. Mime also gives you the opportunity to further your own sense of self-expression. Group work and partnering will develop your ability to work cooperatively and productively with others.

Just as cross training benefits athletes, it enriches dancers. Modern dance, for example, introduces you to exciting new movement shapes and possibilities. Jazz and tap can also stretch you to think and move in different ways.

Poses from a Minuet

To perform this minuet, imagine that you have been transported back in time to France, during the reign of King Louis XIV. In Louis' opulent and mannered court, the graceful carriage of young nobles was painstakingly cultivated by the dancing masters. Picture yourself elegantly attired and dancing in a ballroom illuminated by a thousand shimmering candles.

Pas de Deux

Pas de deux is a partnership that relies on mutual trust and respect. At its most inspired, it conveys a range and depth of emotions that makes it unparalleled in its capacity to touch audiences. To begin, the emphasis is on supported *adage*, where the boy learns to place the girl exactly on balance. You will also work together to coordinate your movements and develop harmony of line. Support your partner by communicating your feelings, remaining positive, and providing encouragement, as the artistic rapport between couples is what gives *pas de deux* its power.

In time, you will progress to lifts where you and your partner synchronize your preparations and then jump or lift in unison. As you watch the *grand pas de deux* which crowns many classical ballets, you will be captivated by the stunning displays of virtuosity. Notice, however, that it is the couple's use of eye contact and their empathic response to each other that ultimately provides the audience with a truly engrossing theatrical experience.

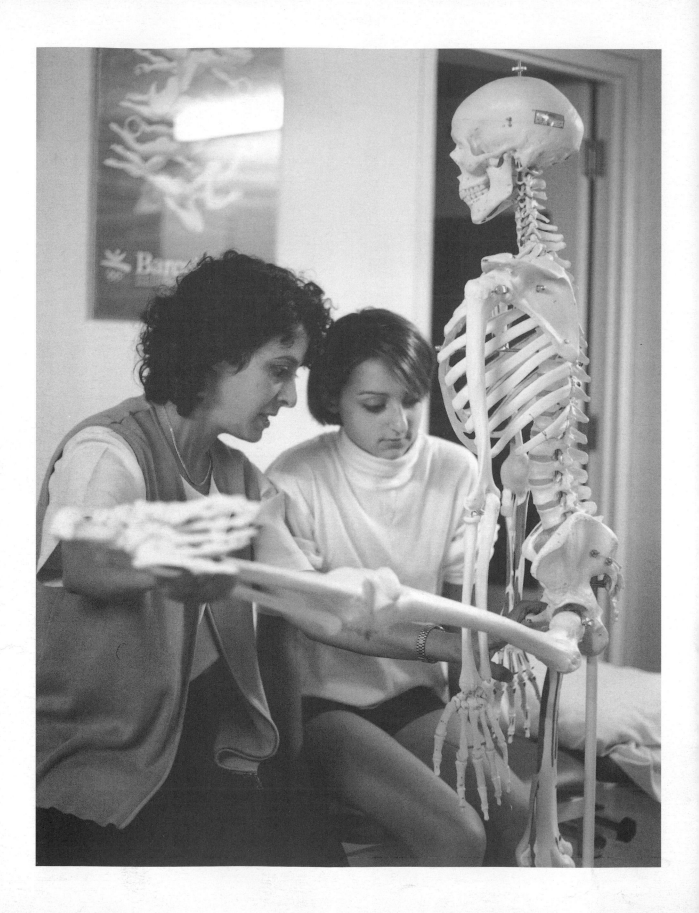

CHAPTER THREE
The Healthy Dancer

In this unique and demanding art
form, dancers must blend artistry and
athleticism. Flexibility, muscle
strength, endurance and
cardiovascular fitness support the
artistry we see on stage. Your dance
teacher will gradually introduce you
to a variety of exercises. Some are
designed to improve your general
fitness level, and others are ballet-
specific. Included is a sampling of
basic exercises that will benefit all
young dancers. Your teacher should
also help you to understand which
exercises will most benefit your
particular physique.

Once you understand the basic body-conditioning exercises that you have been taught, repeat them outside of class. Make a schedule and fit them into your daily routine. Always train within your physical capabilities, stretch only when you are well warmed up, and be particularly sensible as you go through growth spurts. As your pattern of growth is genetically determined, you and your peers will grow at different times and at your own pace. Your bones grow first, and then your muscles and ligaments adjust. During these periods it is quite natural to feel tighter and less coordinated. Thoughtful exercising, however, will help to ease these symptoms.

Just as a professional athlete combines a balanced exercise program with sensible eating habits, so should you, in order to meet the demands of ballet training. As your body is your sole instrument and medium for self-expression, it must be nurtured and respected. As you grow, it is extremely important to balance your intake of nutrients. You probably know that calcium is required for bone growth, but do you also know that proteins, carbohydrates and fats are all essential to long-term health? A nutritious snack, to have before ballet class, is an important addition to your dance bag. Choose a bagel with cheese, fruit, or yogurt, and avoid sugary snacks that give you a quick but short-lived burst of energy. Remember also to drink water before, during and after training to stay well hydrated. Waiting until you are thirsty is too late, as you have already compromised your body's ability to perform.

Dancing is good for everyone. What you learn in ballet class transfers well to other athletic pursuits. As it works your legs symmetrically, ballet can, for example, help you kick a soccer ball equally well with either foot. The elevation you develop will increase your vertical jump in basketball, and a heightened sense of balance will give you an edge in skating and gymnastics.

Enjoy your dance training, and remember that just as you can excel at sports without wanting to become a professional athlete, you can gain tremendous satisfaction from dancing without aspiring to dance professionally. Regardless of your body type, ballet training will teach healthy posture, promote concentration, develop self-discipline, and give you a lifelong appreciation of this art form. It may lead to a career in a related field, make you into a dedicated patron of the arts, or enable you to excel in other dance forms. If you dream of a career in ballet, talk to your parents and teacher about auditioning for a well-recognized professional school. Choose one that nurtures young dancers with care, and one that has produced many outstanding artists.

Postural Alignment

Your training needs to be grounded in healthy posture. If, when standing with your legs outwardly rotated, you are able to drop a plumb line from your earlobe to the centre of your ankle, you are standing correctly. The line should pass through the vertebrae in your neck, the centre of your shoulder joint, the midline of your trunk, and then through your thigh bone, knee joint and calf.

Certainly every part of your body needs to be correctly aligned; however, the positioning of the pelvis is often thought of as the key to good stance. It should be positioned to maintain and slightly elongate the normal curves of the back without exaggerating or flattening them. It may help to imagine that, if a light shone down from your tailbone, it would illuminate the spot where your heels meet in first position.

Your head should be poised on your spine in a relaxed and well-balanced position. With your chin parallel to the floor, your eye level will naturally include your audience. Keep approximately two-thirds of your body weight placed over the balls of your feet, and take care to divide it equally between your first and fifth metatarsals. You are now ready to move easily and dynamically in any direction.

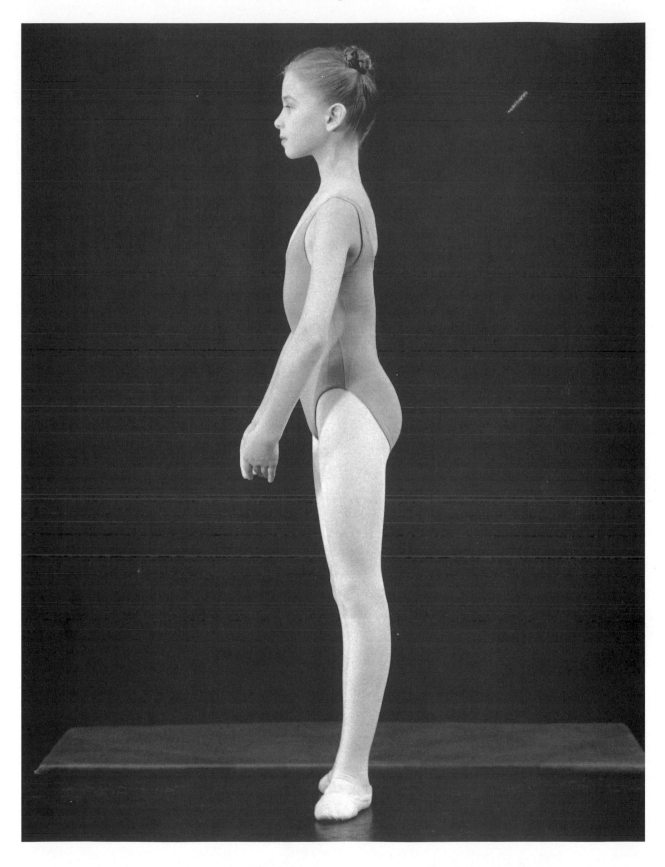

Abdominals

Abdominals

Strong abdominal muscles give you a secure centre from which to extend yourself in more challenging movements. They also provide excellent back insurance. To find these muscles, put your hand on your pelvis, just below your bikini line, and laugh or cough. To activate them, try these three steps. Begin by drawing your low abdominal muscles together, as if to narrow your pelvis, then lift them up toward your navel and press them back toward your spine. Keep your pelvis in a neutral position, and isolate your hard work to your abdominals. Your ribs and shoulders should remain relaxed, and you should be breathing normally.

When you can isolate and activate these muscles, you are ready to involve them in increasingly difficult tasks. Engage your abdominals, then raise your bent legs off the floor, to a 90-degree angle. Slowly lower one leg until your toe touches the floor, and then return it to the raised position. Alternate legs and increase the repetitions as you gain strength. Avoid arching your back, or pushing it into the floor. The farther you extend your limbs from the centre, the harder your abdominals must work. After mastering this exercise, try extending one leg *en l'air* and then the other, to further strengthen your abdominals. Use your imagination to vary these exercises by, for example, moving your gesture leg sideways.

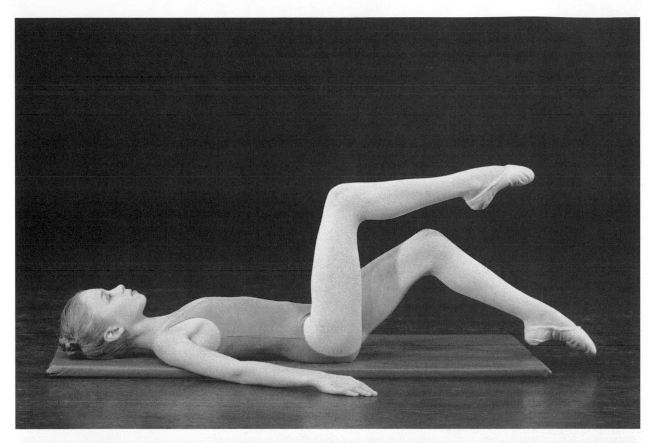

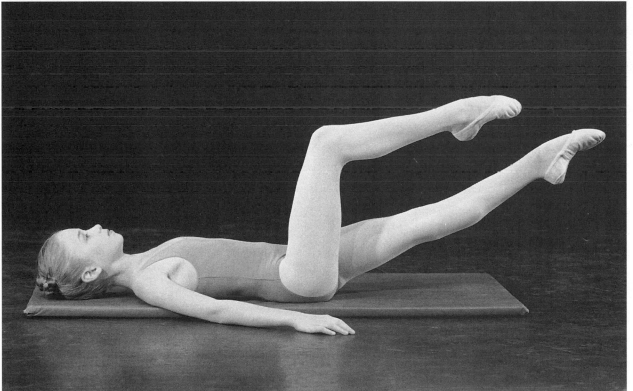

Turnout muscles

Turnout

Turnout is basic to ballet. It affords you a stable base, a large range of movement of the leg in the hip socket, elongated muscle use, and aesthetically pleasing lines. At first glance, it may appear that turnout originates with the feet. In fact, nothing could be further from the truth. Turnout is initiated at the top of each leg by a group of six small muscles, located deep underneath your seat, that connect your thigh to your pelvis. Dance teachers often refer to these as your deep outward rotators or turnout muscles.

The degree of turnout you can achieve is largely determined by your bone structure; however, strong rotator muscles will enable you to achieve your personal best. Always remind yourself that turnout is a movement, and that many other muscles must join in to support this action throughout your entire leg.

When standing, align your tailbone directly over your heels, and keep your knees centred over your feet as you work your turnout muscles. Remember that turnout must be shared equally between both

legs, even when they are performing very different tasks.

During your first ballet lessons, do not be alarmed if turnout is not even mentioned. Good posture comes first and many excellent exercises, from *pliés* and *tendus* to *sautés* and *galops*, may be started with the legs in a parallel or neutral alignment.

In the simple exercise pictured above, use your lower abdominal and trunk muscles to steady yourself while working your deep turnout muscles. Rotate the head of your thigh bone in its hip socket, and allow this action to initiate a change in your gesture leg. Be careful to keep your hips in line, and avoid rocking back and forth as you turn out and in. You should feel the muscle work around the area of your sitting bone.

To build a healthy physique, always balance your exercises. As ballet stresses turnout, include in your body-conditioning routine exercises that stretch, or turn in, your deep rotator muscles. Your ballet teacher will be able to introduce you to some movements that will address this particular need.

Feet

To mobilize your feet and ankles and explore their full range of movement, flex and then extend into a fully stretched position. Roll through quarter, half, and three-quarter pointe, as you will need to use this sequence in your classwork. Keep your toes strong and long as they arc through the air to complete the line. Maximize your pointe by doming the small, intrinsic muscles in the metatarsal area of your foot. If you experience some cramping as you find and engage these muscles,

do not be alarmed. This is a normal reaction. To ease the cramp, press your fingers into its centre and bravely massage it out.

Never scrunch your toes, or jam your heel toward your ankle. To further strengthen your feet, use an elasticized band or towel to supply a slight resistance as you stretch. Well stretched feet allow you to achieve aesthetically pleasing lines that taper to a fine pointe, and extend past your toes into the air around you.

The Back

To strengthen your back muscles, lie face down with your fingers under your forehead, and your elbows in line with your ears. Begin by activating your abdominal muscles, and lifting your navel off the mat. Then slightly lift your upper body, arms and head to work the muscles right down the length of your spine. Reach your shoulder blades and elbows away from your spine and relax the tops of your shoulders as you lift. Hold this position for approximately five seconds. Begin with ten repetitions, or reduce this to the number you can do while keeping your abdominals engaged.

In this back extension, begin, once again, by using your abdominals. Then, moving vertebra by vertebra from the top of your head, lift your spine into a long and sweeping curve. Keep your shoulders wide, and your breathing rhythmical. Lower by rolling through your spine, but this time from bottom to top. Do not release your abdominals until you are completely finished. To balance this extension, sit back on your heels and round your back as fully as possible.

A healthy back is both strong and flexible, and a good ballet teacher will balance your classwork and body-conditioning exercises to develop these characteristics. During backbends, imagine that you are lengthening your spine, and that you have a bubble of air between each vertebra. Do not burst any bubbles, particularly through your lower spine, as it tends to be more mobile and prone to "hinging," or compressing, as you bend.

Hamstrings

This exercise strengthens and stretches your hamstrings. Keep your back and pelvis well aligned as you lift one thigh toward your chest and clasp your hands around it. Now stretch your knee without disturbing your back alignment. If this is too awkward, place a towel around your leg and hold one end in each hand. To lengthen your hamstring, gently pull your leg toward your chest. When you feel a stretch, hold the position for approximately one minute. Then gently push your leg into your hands, as if to lower it, for approximately six seconds. Do these two movements three times in all. In this, as in other exercises, you should push yourself until you experience a stretch that may feel uncomfortable, but not painful. Do this exercise with your legs in parallel and outwardly rotated alignments.

Strong hamstrings will help you to align your standing leg correctly, jump high, and lift your gesture leg in *arabesque* and *attitude derrière*. Lengthened hamstrings keep your lower back well-positioned, and permit you to develop higher extensions in *devant* and *à la seconde* alignments.

Stamina

Aerobic cardiovascular conditioning improves your ability to sustain physically demanding activities. Try to find time to engage in continuous movement for three or more minutes, several times in a row. Keep moving in between these three-minute workouts, to keep your heart rate up, and incorporate them into your daily routine at least three times a week.

Skipping to music promotes coordination, musicality and powerful *allegro* work, in addition to building cardiovascular fitness. Stretch your feet fully *en l'air*, then *plié* with your knees over your toes and your feet spread into the floor. Try skipping in all directions, jumping from one foot to the other, and hopping on one leg. With sound body mechanics, skipping is both good for you and fun. Can you remember any skipping songs to sing, in order to increase your fitness level even further?

A well-trained aerobic system will let you enjoy your dancing more, as you will find that longer sequences become less taxing and fatiguing. During performances your breathing will be easier, and your muscles less apt to "tie up." As a result, you will be better able to remain focussed on your overall presentation.

Hands

Development of fine muscle control is exceptionally important for you as a dancer. Be aware of your extremities. Can you move each of your fingers separately without tensing or disturbing your other digits? Control in the right places allows you to relax and move with artistry. Your hands should speak to the audience. Relaxed, sensitive hands are articulate, while tense or vague hands seem to mumble unintelligibly.

In this exercise, gently bring the heels of your hands, then your palms, and finally your fingers together. Softly push away with your fingertips to separate your hands, draw a heart in the air with your middle fingers, and begin again.

In Exultation

Choreography by David Allan (class of 1975); music by George Frideric Handel.

NBS, 1988, with Alexander Ritter (class of 1987, Soloist, New York City Ballet and American Ballet Theatre).

CHAPTER FOUR

Performing

Ballet is a performing art. The best performers enrich our spirits, and conjure up within us previously unimagined possibilities, thoughts and feelings. Their ability to interpret roles fills their movements with shape and expression.

Communicating through movement, and using the unique and evocative language of ballet to express yourself, is a wondrously powerful and original experience.

If you dream of being on stage, choose a studio that offers this opportunity and go to, or watch a video of, their latest production. The show should run smoothly, and the young dancers should perform expressively, while presenting their work with clarity and confidence. It is important to realize, however, that performing can take many forms and be extremely satisfying—whether you are "onstage" in your living room or in an elegant theatre. All performances involve contact with an audience, and while many students are energized by the prospect of performing, some are happiest dancing on their own. A sensitive teacher will recognize your readiness to perform and will prepare you well for each occasion, from parents' days, to examinations, to recitals.

A person who plans and arranges the steps in a dance is called a choreographer. Many great choreographers continue to contribute to the vast and diverse repertoire that exists today:

productions that challenge and reward artists and audiences alike. As your knowledge of dance grows, you may find that certain movements trigger your imagination and inspire you to make up your own dances. Perhaps sounds, from the pulse of a single drum to the rich textures of a full orchestra, are what motivate you. The life of your piece could also spring from a particular story, poem, picture or sculpture. If you are fascinated by the total theatrical experience, you may want to work with friends to mount a production that uses costumes, make-up, scenery, and lighting. If so, allow yourself plenty of time for reflection and practice, and have at least one full dress rehearsal before performing.

In this chapter you will find pictures of young dancers and mature artists, trained at the National Ballet School (NBS), performing in a number of ballets. Like you, they are exploring the physical and spiritual nature of dance, and cultivating their love of ballet as a performing art.

A Month in the Country
Choreography by Sir Frederick Ashton;
music by Frédéric Chopin.
The National Ballet of Canada
(NBOC), 1995, with Karen Kain (class
of 1969, Artist in Residence and former
Principal Dancer at the NBOC).

This English masterpiece was acquired by the NBOC as a 25th anniversary present for Karen Kain. Based on a play by Ivan Turgenev, its richly drawn characters provide deeply satisfying opportunities for mature artists and ingénues alike. The story focusses on the mistress of the house, who finds herself caught up in a love triangle with an engaging young tutor and her pretty, spirited ward.

The Nutcracker

Choreography and libretto by James Kudelka (class of 1973, Artistic Director, the NBOC, former Principal Dancer, Les Grands Ballets Canadiens, and Soloist, the NBOC); music by Peter Ilyich Tchaikovsky.

The NBOC, 1996, with Victoria Bertram (class of 1963, Principal Character Artist, the NBOC), Jeremy Ransom (class of 1978, Principal Dancer, the NBOC), and NBS students Susan McElhinney and Warren Benns.

This sumptuous production features 66 eager young dancers, as well as the voices of the Canadian Children's Opera Chorus. Set in nineteenth-century Russia, it relates the magical Christmas Eve adventures of Marie and her brother Misha. The wonder begins when Marie receives a nutcracker as a present from her mysterious Uncle Nikolai. Pictured here are Nikolai and his old mare, who do a dance together, much to everyone's surprise and delight. Later, the children journey to the secret kingdom of the Sugar Plum Fairy. There they meet their beloved Baba, who has been transformed into a Duchess, and is shown here shepherding her little lambs.

Concerto Barocco

Choreography by George Balanchine; music by Johann Sebastian Bach. NBS, 1995, with Jamie Tapper (class of 1994, Soloist, the NBOC).

This ballet is rooted in the musical structure of Bach's *Double Violin Concerto in D Minor*. Pictured here is one of two female soloists whose movements counterpoint Bach's melodies, and develop the orchestral themes purely through dance.

Here We Come

Choreography by Erik Bruhn; music by Morton Gould.
NBS, 1978, with John Alleyne (class of 1978, Artistic Director, Ballet B.C. and former Soloist, the NBOC and Stuttgart Ballet).

The young men at NBS were challenged and inspired by Erik Bruhn's teaching, and thrilled with this light-hearted and stirring piece he created especially for them.

Chopiniana/Les Sylphides
Choreography by Michel Fokine; music by Frédéric Chopin.
NBS, 1996, with Misako Yanai (class of 1996, Dancer, Stuttgart Ballet) and Avinoam Silverman (class of 1996, Dancer, the NBOC).

This intensely romantic ballet marked a clear departure from earlier Russian ballets since it was not based on a storyline, and used music not specifically written for the ballet. Set in a moonlit glade, the ballet evokes an atmosphere of dream-like beauty as a young poet is visited by luminous, ethereal beings who represent the intangible expression of his creative musings. He is seen here dancing a tender pas de deux with one of his muses.

Swan Lake

Choreography by Marius Petipa and Lev Ivanov; music by Peter Ilyich Tchaikovsky.

NBS, 1986, with Jennifer Fournier (class of 1985, Principal Dancer, the NBOC) and Stephen Legate (class of 1985, Principal Dancer, the San Francisco Ballet).

In this compelling story of true love, the full range of our emotions is captured by the timeless struggle between good and evil. The most fully realized of the romantic ballets, it continues to entrance audiences and provide a touchstone for all ballerinas who perform the dual roles of Odette, the gentle and lyrical white swan, and Odile, the dazzling, yet destructive black swan.

Yondering

Choreography by John Neumeier; music by Stephen C. Foster.
NBS, 1996, with Alison Kappes (class of 1998, Apprentice, Hamburg Ballet) and Mike Spendlove (class of 1996, Dancer, Hong Kong Ballet).

The students at NBS were most fortunate to have this ballet choreographed for them. The term "Yondering" originated in the early American west and meant going "over yonder" or into the unknown. The ballet journeys through seven songs, and pictured here is a moment from "Molly! Do You Love Me?" which explores the endearing awkwardness of first love.

Four Last Songs

Choreography by Rudi Van Danzig; music by Richard Strauss.
NBS, 1981, with (left to right): Anthony Randazzo (class of 1980, Principal Dancer, the NBOC and the San Francisco Ballet), Sabina Allemann (class of 1979, Principal Dancer, the San Francisco Ballet), Rex Harrington (class of 1981, Principal Dancer, the NBOC), Martine Lamy (class of 1982, Principal Dancer, the NBOC), Jeffrey Kirk (class of 1979, Principal Dancer, Hamburg Ballet), Kim Lightheart (class of 1979, Principal Dancer, the NBOC), Donald Acevedo (class of 1980, Dancer, the NBOC), Anne Adair (class of 1981, Principal Dancer, Ballet Met and the Royal Danish Ballet) and Serge Lavoie (class of 1981, Principal Dancer, the NBOC).

This ballet was presented to NBS in 1979, by its choreographer, in honour of the school's 20th anniversary. It deals with the themes of separation and death in a haunting, but ultimately consoling way. In the fourth song, "At Dusk," the reunited couples find themselves moving forward together, as if caught in the current of a powerful river.

Pas de Deux from Le Corsaire
Choreography by Marius Petipa; music
by Ricardo Drigo.
NBS, 1995, with Bei Di Sheng
(class of 1995, Dancer, the NBOC) and
Jhe Russell (class of 1994, Dancer, the
NBOC).

Based on Lord Byron's poem *The*
Corsair, this sensational *pas de deux* is
part of a seldom seen, full length
ballet. Here, a beautiful Greek girl
who has been sold into slavery
dances with a dynamic and
impassioned male slave.

Manon

Choreography by Kenneth MacMillan;
music by Jules Massenet.
The NBOC, 1996, with Martine Lamy
and Johan Persson (class of 1989,
Soloist, the NBOC).

Based on a novel written in 1773, this ballet explores the effect of wealth, love and corruption on a young woman's life. Here we see Manon hesitate before she removes the elegant bracelet, which is the last remaining symbol of her prosperous life as a courtesan. She renounces this affluence to join Des Grieux, a young man whose obsessive love for her lures him into crime.

Giselle

Choreography by Peter Wright after Coralli/Perrot/Petipa; music by Adolphe Adam.

The NBOC, 1992, with Kimberly Glasco (class of 1979, Principal Dancer, the NBOC).

This enduring classic is, for many balletomanes, the greatest of the romantic ballets, always offering ballerinas the opportunity to interpret it anew. Giselle is at once real, as an innocent village girl, and then, after her tragic death, illusory as a Wili, or spiritual embodiment of a betrothed maiden who has died before her wedding day. Here Giselle, heartbroken in love, is overcome with grief, and losing her reason, she picks at an imaginary flower, playing out the game of "he loves me, he loves me not."

The Actress

Choreography by James Kudelka; music by Frédéric Chopin.
The NBOC, 1994, with Karen Kain and Rex Harrington.

Created for Karen Kain, this ballet is based on a series of vignettes in which a mature, elegant woman recalls a day in her life as a ballerina.

Le Charme de L'Impossible
Choreography by Peggy Baker; music by Mark Kolt.
NBS, 1992, with Sabra Perry (class of 1991, Dancer, the NBOC).

One of Canada's pre-eminent modern dancers, Peggy Baker is also artist-in-residence at NBS. Senior students benefit greatly from her classes in which both their movement horizons and their

understanding of the spiritual dimensions of dance are expanded.

Jardin de Alegrias

*Choreography by Susana; music by
Antonio Robledo.*
*NBS, 1995, with Ana-Maria Lucaciu
(class of 1995, Dancer, the Royal Danish
Ballet).*

Choreographed especially for the students at NBS, this piece is based on one of several rhythmic forms of flamenco, called alegrias. These dances are characterized by their freedom of form, and by their spontaneous nature that gives each dancer the opportunity to develop an individual style, based on the fundamental technique.

Glossary

A

Adage At ease. Slow, sustained movements designed to develop grace, sense of line and balance.

Air, en l' In the air.

Allegro Brisk and lively. All jumping steps.

Aplomb Poise and assurance. Control of movement in a vertical plane.

Arabesque A pose on one leg, with the other fully stretched and extended behind the body.

Arrière, en Travelling backward.

Assemblé Assembled. A jump in which the legs are brought together in the air.

Attitude A pose on one leg, with the other bent at the knee and extended in front of or behind the body.

Avant, en Travelling forward.

B

Balancé A swinging or rocking step.

Ballon Bounce. The easy, light, rebounding quality required in jumps.

Barre The horizontal bar on which dancers rest their hands during preliminary exercises.

Bas, en Low.

Battement Beating.

Battement, grand A movement in which one leg is thrown high into the air.

Battement, petit A small, quick action of the lower leg, in which the gesture foot swings slightly sideways and then back to contact the ankle of the standing leg.

Battement fondu An exercise in which both legs bend and stretch smoothly and simultaneously.

Battement frappé A movement in which one foot quickly strikes out from *cou-de-pied* into a fully extended position.

(Battement tendu...)

Battement tendu A movement in which one foot slides along the ground to a fully stretched position.

Battement tendu jeté A movement in which one foot is thrown just off the ground.

Batterie All jumps in which the legs beat together.

Bras Arm.

C

Changé Changed.

Choreography The art of composing ballets.

Cou-de-pied Neck of the foot. The position of the gesture foot when placed at the ankle of the standing leg.

Couru, pas Running step.

Croisé A position of the body or pose, taken on a slight angle to the audience, in which the dancer's lines appear crossed.

D

Dedans, en   Inward. The inward circling of the gesture leg, from back to front, or turning movements that revolve toward the standing leg.

Dehors, en   Outward. The outward circling of the gesture leg, from front to back, or turning movements that revolve away from the standing leg.

Demi   Half.

Derrière   Behind.

Devant   In front.

Développé   Developed. The unfolding of the gesture leg into a fully extended position.

E

Ecarté   Thrown wide apart. A pose in which the dancer stands at a slight angle to the audience, with the gesture leg in second position.

Echappé   Escaped. A movement in which the legs "escape" from a closed to an open position.

Effacé   Shaded. A position of the body or pose, taken on a slight angle to the audience, in which the dancer's lines appear uncrossed or open.

Enchaînement   Linking. A combination that links a series of steps together.

Entrechat   Interweaving. A jump in which the dancer's legs beat together in the air.

Epaulement   Shouldering.

F

Face, en   Facing. A position of the body, taken facing the audience.

Fondu   Melted.

Frappé   Struck.

G

Galop   A travelling step done forward, sideways, or backward to the line of dance.

Glissade   A gliding step used most commonly as a linking or preparatory movement.

Grand   Large.

J

Jeté   Thrown. A jump from one foot to the other.

O

Ouvert   Open.

P

Pas de deux   A dance for two.

Passé   Passed.

Penché   Inclined or tilted.

Petit   Small.

Pirouette   A whirl or turn on one leg.

Place, sur   On the spot.

Plié   Bent. A bending of the knee(s).

Pointe tendue   A position in which the gesture leg and foot are fully stretched, while the tips of the toes stay in contact with the ground.

Pointes, sur les   Standing on pointe, on the tips of the toes.

Port de bras   Carriage of the arms. The graceful movement of the arms from one position to another.

Porté   Carried.

R

Relevé   A movement in which the dancer rises onto half or full pointe.

Repertoire   The works that are performed by a ballet company.

Rond de jambe par terre   A circle of the leg on the ground.

S

Sauté   Jumped.

Seconde, à la   To the second position.

T

Temps levé   Time lifted. A basic jump.

Tendu   Stretched.

Terre, à   On the ground.

Terre à terre   Ground to ground. A jump in which the feet barely leave the ground.

Tour   Turn.

Tournant, en   Turning.

Turnout   Outward rotation of the legs. A movement initiated from the tops of the thighs.

Tutu   A tulle skirt that may be cut short (classical style) or long (romantic style).

Acknowledgments

The National Ballet School would like to thank Deborah Bowes for writing and arranging this book.

Deborah Bowes is indebted to all of her colleagues at NBS for their support and encouragement. In particular: Mavis Staines for her advice and editorial assistance; Deborah Hess for her comments and help in posing the dancers; Lindsay Melcher for her contributions to "The Healthy Dancer"; Caroline O'Brien for designing the dancewear; Mary Ann West, Scott Martin and Ian McMaster for organizing and lighting the photo shoots; and Carole Beaulieu for coordinating the project with the publisher. Additionally, Deborah gratefully acknowledges the following NBS staff who gave so generously of their time and expertise: Carol and Larry Beevers, Carole Chadwick, Marjorie Clarkson, Jeannette Edissi-Collins, Elaine Fisher, Ralph Hamelmann, Stephen Johnson, Beverley Miller, Sergiu Stefanschi, and Carole Wagland. Finally, Deborah has been most appreciative of her husband Philip Stevens' computer skills.

Photo Credits

Except where indicated below, photos by
Lydia Pawelak.

John Alleyne: page 125.
D. Brian Campbell: page 124, 137.
Jeanette Edissi-Collins: page 101, 118, 136.
Barry Gray: page 129.
Ralph Hamelmann: page 98.
Robert Nelson: page 6.
Andrew Oxenham: page 121, 132, 133.
Johan Persson: page 127, 133.
David Street: page 122.
Cylla von Tiedemann: page 119, 123.
John Wong: page 127.

Photo Captions

Page 12, NBS Guest teacher Annette Av
Paul guides Alexis Maragozis.
Page 13, NBS pianist Craig Wingrove
works with a group of young dancers.
Page 14, NBS staff member Sergiu
Stefanschi instructs Lawrence Haegert.
Page 98, NBS Manager of
Physiotherapy and Health Services,
Lindsay Melcher, chats with Nicole
Papadopoulos.

Index

Deborah Bowes

Deborah Bowes graduated from the National Ballet School in 1965, and from the University of Victoria in 1970. She trained as a teacher under Betty Oliphant, NBS's founding principal, and has taught boys and girls and teachers in training at NBS for over 25 years. As a guest teacher, Ms. Bowes has taught most recently at the Royal Danish Ballet School. An Examiner for the Cecchetti Branch of the Imperial Society of Teachers of Dancing, she lives in Toronto with her husband and two sons.

Lydia Pawelak

Lydia Pawelak was born and raised in Belgium, where she earned a Degree in Photography. In 1995 she immigrated to Canada. Currently based in Montreal, she specializes in performing arts and travel photography with clients such as the National Ballet of Canada. Her work has appeared in publications all over the world, including *The New York Times*. For further information about Ms. Pawelak, and additional examples of her work, visit her at www.generation.net/~lightmo